Sugar Inspirations

Wedding Flowers

CYNTHIA VENN

Published 1995 by Merehurst Limited
Ferry House, 51–57 Lacy Road, Putney,
London SW15 1PR

Copyright © Merehurst Limited 1995
ISBN 1-85391-452-5

A catalogue record for this book is available from the
British Library.

Editor: Helen Southall
Designer: Rita Wüthrich
Photography by Ferguson Hill

Typeset by Servis Filmsetting Ltd, Manchester
Colour separation by P & W Graphics Pty Ltd, Singapore
Printed in Italy by Milanostampa SpA

Contents

Introduction

Flowers are a very important part of any celebration;

as they are frequently used to express love and appreciation,

a wedding without flowers is inconceivable.

Choosing flowers

The theme of the wedding is important in determining the choice of flowers for the cake, and the following points should be considered:

● The flowers the bride has chosen to carry.

● The general colour scheme.

● Flowers on the cake should be compatible with those in the bride's and bridesmaids' bouquets.

● The sprays of flowers on the wedding cake can be similar in shape to the bride's bouquet.

● Although the modern trend is to display flowers in natural, informal arrangements, flowers for bridal cakes are still generally arranged in traditional sprays and posies.

All serious cake decorators get great satisfaction from making beautiful flowers and displaying them attractively; some of these displays are a work of art in themselves and take many hours to create. Some of the flowers in this book use shortcuts to help cut down on the time required to make them. Nevertheless, they all make the most beautiful of cake decorations.

One of the delights of flower making is the huge variety of flowers you can make. Even flowers of the same species can vary in colour and shape. Before adding colour to your flowers, consult a botanical reference book; you may not be able to imitate nature, but you can try to make your flowers as true to life as possible.

Displaying flowers

Sugar flowers can be displayed on cakes in a variety of ways:
● The stems can be bound together with floral tape and pushed into a neat plastic posy holder, which has previously been pushed into the cake.
● The spray may be laid in position after the cake has been assembled on its stand or pillars. If preferred, the spray can be secured with a small amount of royal icing under the stem.

● Individual flower and leaf stems can be set in a cushion of sugarpaste in a natural arrangement. The whole display can then be lifted off the cake before cutting.
● Trailing flowers can be wound around the cake stand.
● Flowers can be set in a cushion of sugarpaste on the cake board.

Flowers should be given enough space to ensure that none are hidden. The addition of a few leaves contrasts well with pale-coloured flowers, accentuating their delicacy and avoiding an otherwise bland effect (see page 15). Whilst an 'open' bouquet looks better than a tight bunch of flowers, it is necessary to hide the 'mechanics' of the spray. This is not easy as sugar flowers are not pliable, as fresh or silk flowers would be, and can break.

Careful positioning of larger flowers is advisable to help cover some of the stem. Some decorators use ribbon loops or tulle to fill in unsightly gaps which are too small for a flower; whilst this is acceptable in moderation for wedding bouquets, small sprigs of lilac (hand-modelled in sugar) or dried material (such as baby's breath or gypsophila) make the bouquet look much more realistic and show more creativity.

Equipment

It is very important to choose equipment carefully to avoid buying unnecessary items and making expensive mistakes. Don't be tempted to think that a complete set of equipment will immediately make you an expert. The truth is quite the opposite; only patience and practice will make an expert capable of making exquisite flowers with the minimum of tools.

Start by buying the essential equipment required for the flowers you wish to make, and slowly add items as you need them, taking advice from more experienced flower-makers if possible. Always buy the best quality you can afford as good tools will last a lifetime and help you achieve good results; poor-quality tools might well be cheaper, but they will cause constant frustration.

Flower Paste

I prefer to make my own paste from one of the recipes on page 46. Both of these pastes give good results and are easy to work with. It is now possible to buy ready-made flower paste (also called 'petal' or 'gum' paste) but the quality does vary quite a lot. Try several brands until you find the one which suits you best.

Scissors

Fine, pointed scissors, preferably the cranked type, are an essential item. The blades of these scissors are angled to make precision cutting easier. For cutting wires, an old pair of strong kitchen scissors is helpful.

Wires

Ready-taped wires are the most convenient; the most useful sizes are gauges 24, 26, 28, 30 and 33.

Modelling tools

There are several brands on the market which can be bought in sets or individually. Some of the tools in the sets are not used as often as the others but important ones are:
- A ball tool, sometimes referred to as a 'dog bone tool'.
- A tool which has a veiner one end and a spoon-shaped opposite end for fluting.
- A pointed tool with ridges.

Check carefully for a smooth finish on the ball tool – this is essential to avoid tearing the delicate paste. Beginners should take advice from a teacher or reputable supplier before buying, if possible.

Cutters

These must be well made and absolutely level for even cutting. When the cutter is not level, no amount of perseverance will enable you to cut your petal/leaf with a good, clean edge.

Polythene bags

Small sturdy bags are ideal for storing small amounts of paste which have already been coloured.

Palette

This is useful when mixing together paste colours and/or dusting powders.

Drying stand

When flowers are complete, leave them to dry in a purpose-built flower stand, or push the wires into a piece of polystyrene or florist's oasis where the flowers can safely be left to dry. If a flower has heavy, floppy petals, leave it upside-down to firm up before standing upright.

Other essential items

Rolling board (preferably non-stick) and small rolling pin;

good-quality paintbrushes in several sizes, including a very fine one;

special dusting brush (thicker than a paintbrush but with soft bristles);

cocktail sticks, preferably wooden as these do not slip on the paste (choose sticks which are nicely rounded);

special rigid foam for tooling petals;

stamens – fine, yellow ones, and white ones which can also be dusted any other shade;

modelling knife;

paste food colourings;

dusting powders;

cranked fine-bladed palette knife;

fine-pointed tweezers;

round-ended tweezers;

veiners.

Three=tier Rose Cake

Roses are an ever=popular choice for brides;

the embroidered rose border on this=three tier cake continues the rose theme set

by the moulded sprays on top.

Materials
15cm (6 inch), 20cm
(8 inch), and 25cm
(10 inch) round cakes
Apricot glaze
2.25kg (4½lb) almond
paste
Clear alcohol (vodka or
gin) for brushing
3.25kg (6½lb)
sugarpaste
250g (8oz) royal icing
Food colourings
1cm (½ inch) ribbon
2.5mm (⅛ inch) ribbon

Equipment
20cm (8 inch), 28cm
(11 inch), and 36cm
(14 inch) round cake
boards
Masking tape
Scriber
Paper piping bags
Plain piping tubes (nos.
0 and 1)
Paintbrush

Flowers
2 rose bouquets (see
page 12)
1 cake-top ornament
(see page 14)

Preparing the cakes

1 Brush the cakes with apricot glaze and cover with the almond paste. Leave for 2–3 days for the paste to firm up.

2 Brush the almond paste with alcohol, and cover the cakes with sugarpaste. Leave to dry. Cover the cake boards with sugarpaste and leave to set hard. Place the cakes on the boards.

Making the rose border

3 Make a template for the largest cake by cutting a strip of greaseproof or non-stick paper long enough to go all round the cake and the same depth as the cake. Make two more templates for the other two cakes in the same way.

4 Trace the rose border design from page 14 on to the templates, repeating it as many times as necessary. Wrap the templates around the cakes, securing them with tape. Using the point of a scriber, scribe over the outlines to mark the fine lines of the pattern on to the surface of each cake.

5 Colour quantities of royal icing pale pink and green. Work the design in brush embroidery by piping the outline of one petal or leaf at a time (using a no. 0 or 1 tube) and evenly brushing with a damp paint-brush through to the base of the petal or leaf. Unless the section you are working on is very small, you will need to pipe an additional heavier line at the tip to give sufficient icing to brush through. Add a little piping gel (¼ teaspoon per 250g/8oz royal icing) to keep the icing soft enough to brush. Change to a piping bag fitted with a no. 1 tube to pipe the stems in green royal icing.

6 Pipe the scalloped borders above the rose pattern in royal icing to match the colour of the roses, using a piping bag fitted with a no. 1 tube. Pipe a neat snailstrail border around the base of each cake with a no. 1 tube. Arrange rose bouquets on top of the two larger cakes, and the posy ornament on the top cake.

7 Trim the base of each cake, above the piped border, and around each cake board, with ribbon.

Materials
Flower paste (see
page 46)
Hooked 28 gauge wires
Lightly beaten egg white
or gum glue
(see page 47)
Green dusting powder

Equipment
Small knitting needle,
paintbrush
or cocktail stick
Stephanotis cutter
Pointed tool
Small ball
modelling tool
Small star calyx cutter
Paintbrush

1 Make a Mexican hat shape from a pea-sized ball of white flower paste, leaving enough paste to make quite a substantial back to the flower. Thin by rolling with the tip of a small knitting needle, paintbrush handle or cocktail stick. (Stephanotis flowers have quite sturdy, waxy looking blossoms so the paste should not be rolled too thin.) Cut out the flower with a stephanotis cutter. Cut out one at a time, keeping the paste covered with plastic wrap.

2 Press a pointed tool into the centre of the flower. Thin the edges of the petals by stroking with a small ball tool. Indent the front of the petals with a pointed tool or the end of a paintbrush.

3 Push a hooked 28 gauge wire through the flower. Roll the back to form a waist under the petals; the base should be fuller.

4 Colour and roll out a little pale green flower paste, and cut out a small calyx with a star calyx cutter. Slip over the base of the flower and stick with egg white or gum glue. Brush the back of the flower pale green with dusting powder.

Bud
5 Roll a 5mm (¼ inch) ball of white paste into a cone about 1cm (½ inch) long. Keep the base wide and shape the tip into a bud. Insert a 28 gauge wire into the base. Leave to dry.

6 Brush the base of the bud with pale lime green dusting powder. Cut out and position a calyx as in step 4.

Freesia

Freesias come in many lovely colours – red, pink, yellow, purple, white – and the stamens are the same colour as the flower, i.e. if the freesia is to be white, then white stamens should be used.

1 Tape six fine stamens, plus one longer stamen for the pistil, to the end of a 28 gauge wire.

2 Roll a ball of flower paste 8mm (⅓ inch) in diameter, and shape into a cone.

3 Hollow the cone by inserting a cocktail stick into the bulbous end and rotating it to open up the cone into a cylinder, thinning the walls.

4 To form the petals, cut the edge of the cylinder into six sections with small pointed scissors. Cut off the square corners of each petal.

5 Lay each petal in turn over your fingertip and roll the cocktail stick across the front of each one to thin and shape.

6 Insert the wired stamens into the centre of the flower. Thin the back of the flower by rolling between thumb and finger.

7 For a fully open flower, arrange alternate petals towards the centre, with the remaining three petals curving outwards. For a half-

open flower, cup all the petals towards the centre.

8 To make a quick calyx, make two small snips opposite each other at the base of each flower and bud to represent a calyx with two sepals. When dry, colour this green.

9 To make buds, roll a small ball of paste into a long cone, tapering into a narrow tail. Make the smallest buds from green paste and a few larger buds in the same colour as the flowers.

10 To form a spray, tape together buds and flowers, starting with the smallest buds and ending with the fully open flowers.

Materials
6 fine stamens
1 extra long stamen
28 gauge wires
Flower paste
(see page 46)
Green dusting powder

Equipment
Floral tape
Cocktail stick
Small pointed scissors

Lily of the Valley

1 Roll a ball of white flower paste 4mm (⅙ inch) in diameter. Moisten the tip of a stamen with egg white, and insert into the ball.

2 Roll out some white paste very thinly, and cut out shapes with a small lily of the valley cutter.

3 Brush the tip of the ball with egg white and attach the blossom shape. Push a small pointed tool into the centre of the blossom, coaxing the petals into the correct shape. Curve the stamen so that the flower hangs attractively.

4 To make buds, roll tiny balls of paste and stick them to the tips of stamens. Curve the stamen cottons by stroking with a fingernail.

Materials
White flower paste
(see page 46)
Medium stamens
(preferably with
green stems)
Beaten egg white

Equipment
Lily of the valley cutter
Paintbrush
Small pointed tool
26 gauge wire
Floral tape
Scissors

5 Cut a piece of 26 gauge wire. Starting with three buds, tape them to the main wire, leaving short stems. Add five flowers, more buds, flowers and leaves (see page 15).

Rose

This small rose is quick to make and can look very pretty in sprays. A large blossom cutter is used instead of individual rose petal cutters. If you haven't got such a cutter, make a template using the outline opposite. Colour the rose by making it in a pale shade of flower paste, then dusting it with darker tones of the same colour when it is dry. This gives greater depth of colour and a more realistic finish.

Centre
1 Make a cone of flower paste by rolling it until it tapers at one end. Insert a hooked 24 gauge wire. The size of the central cone required depends on the size of the blossom cutter to be used for the petals. To gauge the size, make a cone and lay it in the centre of the cutter with the base in the middle. The tip should be about 5mm (¼ inch) away from the tip of a petal. Allow the cone to dry before adding the petals.

Petals
2 Roll out some flower paste and cut out three blossom shapes. Make 5mm (¼ inch) cuts towards the centre of the blossom shape between the petals to allow the petals more movement. Keep two of the cut-out blossom shapes under plastic wrap to prevent them drying while you work on the third.

3 Cup each petal by working with a ball tool. Stroke the edges to thin them and give some movement, but do not frill.

Violet

1 Roll a 5mm (¼ inch) ball of violet-coloured flower paste into a cone shape. Hollow the wide end by inserting a cocktail stick and rotating it, thinning the sides.

2 With a pair of small pointed scissors, cut the large petal by snipping twice around the edge of the hollowed cone, taking up one third of the rim. Divide the remaining rim into four sections by cutting in half and then cutting each in half again. You should now have one wide petal and four narrow ones.

3 Cut off the square corners of all the petals. Roll a cocktail stick back and forth across the petals to thin them. If they lose their shape, trim with scissors. Roll the back of the flower (the spur) between thumb and finger to make a fine point.

4 The large petal should be at the bottom, and the two small petals at the top should stand upright. The side petals should be drawn in towards the centre, with the tips curved back.

5 Insert a hooked 28 gauge wire into the throat of the flower and exit through the side of the spur, about halfway between petals and tip.

6 Add a short yellow stamen to the centre so that only the tip shows.

Calyx

7 Make a cone from a tiny piece of green paste. Hollow the wide end of the cone and cut the rim into five points with scissors. Thin the points. Moisten the centre and slip over the wire on to the back of the flower, leaving the spur free.

Materials
Flower paste
(see page 46)
Violet and green
food colourings
28 gauge wires
Yellow stamens

Equipment
Cocktail stick
Small pointed scissors

Lily Shower Bouquet

This shower bouquet

displays the large lilies well without being cluttered.

This would look well trailing over the side of a cake.

Flowers
5 sprays of lily of the
valley (see page 10)
4 sprays of stephanotis
(each with 2 flowers,
1 bud and 1 leaf),
see page 8
5 single freesia flowers
(see page 9)
2 small longiflorum
lilies (see page 22)
1 large longiflorum lily
(see page 22)

Equipment
Floral tape
Strong scissors or
wire cutters

1 Tape together two sprays of lily
of the valley. Add one stephanotis spray (two flowers, two leaves)
and one freesia to the right, then add
one more lily of the valley spray to
the left.

2 Add one more stephanotis, with
bud and leaf, to the right. Tape
in one small lily, then one open
freesia to the centre.

3 Add one small lily to the left,
and one stephanotis spray (two
flowers, two leaves and one bud) to
the right. Add one large lily in the
centre of the bouquet.

4 Arrange three single freesias
together and tape them in cen-
trally, followed by one spray of
stephanotis (two flowers, two leaves
and one bud) to the left.

5 Bend two sprays of lily of the
valley with leaves to form return
ends. Tape them on either side of the
main stem. Tape the wires and cut off
neatly.

Longiflorum Lily

Materials
6 'T' shaped stamens
24 gauge wire
Flower paste
(see page 46)
Green food colouring
26 or 28 gauge wire
Beaten egg white or
gum glue (see page 47)
Pale yellow
or lime green food
dusting powder

Equipment
Veining tool
Floral tape
Leaf roller or grooved
rolling board
Thin card
Ball modelling tool
Paintbrush

Stamens

1 Six stamens are required which have a 'T' shaped tip called the anther. It is now possible to buy these, but if you cannot get them, alter a regular medium-sized stamen by rolling a tiny ball of yellow paste into a cigar shape, moistening the tip of the stamen with egg white and inserting it into the centre of the paste, forming a 'T' shape. Repeat to make six.

The Pistil

2 Cut a piece of 24 gauge wire and roll a small piece of pale green paste around the tip, allowing it to travel down the wire until it covers 4cm (1¼ inches). Leave a bulbous tip about 2.5mm (⅛ inch) in diameter at the top.

3 Flatten the top of the pistil and pinch the paste in three places (between your fingers or with tweezers) to form a tricorn shape.

Ovary

4 Attach a very small ball of green paste to the base of the pistil, and mould it around neatly. Using a veining tool, make six indentations in the soft paste, spacing them evenly around the ovary.

5 Set a stamen in each of the six grooves with the heads a little lower than the tip of the pistil. Tape them to the pistil just below the ovary, making sure they are held firmly in position.

Petals

6 Cut six pieces of 26 or 28 gauge white wire. Roll out some white flower paste thinly, leaving a thickened area for the wires. The easiest way to do this is to use a leaf roller with grooves cut in it, or a rolling board with grooves (see Tip).

7 Cut out petals with lily cutters, or trace the petal templates below on to greaseproof or non-stick paper. Cut them out and use them to make two templates of thin card.

8 Cut three paste petals using template A and three using template B. While working on each petal in turn, keep the others covered with plastic wrap. The wider petals (A) form the inside layer; the narrow ones (B) are the outside petals.

9 Starting with one of the wider petals, thin the edges with a ball tool. Vein the petal down the centre, pinching from tip to base to reinforce the crease. Turn the petal over and mark veins on either side of the main vein.

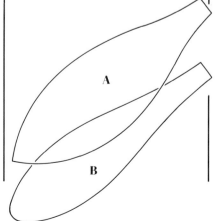

A

B

Pastillage

This mixture can be used for modelling and for making plaques.

500g (1lb/3 cups) icing sugar
1 teaspoon gum tragacanth
3 tablespoons cold water
1½ teaspoons powdered gelatine

1 Put the sugar and gum tragacanth in a heatproof bowl and warm gently in the oven or over a saucepan of hot water.

2 Sprinkle the gelatine on to the water in a small heatproof bowl and leave to soak until all the water is absorbed. Place the bowl in a pan of very hot (but not boiling) water to dissolve the gelatine, stirring from time to time. Check that all the grains of gelatine are dissolved. (Do not boil the mixture as this will destroy the elasticity.)

3 Add the gelatine to the sugar and mix in an electric mixer with a 'K' beater. If a little dry, add a drop more water.

Gum Glue

This is a good alternative adhesive when it is not desirable to use egg white when making flowers.

2 teaspoons gum arabic
4 teaspoons rose water

Put the gum arabic and rose water in a small heatproof pot. Set the pot in a pan of hot water and stir until dissolved.

Extra Strong Gum Glue

This is a very strong, fast-setting 'glue' suitable for sticking together dry petals. It is also very useful for invisibly repairing broken petals, as it can be made exactly the same colour as the flower by using the same paste as a base.

Flower paste (see page 46)
Gum glue (see above) or lightly beaten egg white

Place a small piece of flower paste on a board. Add a drop of gum glue or egg white and mash these together to make a very sticky substance which will dry quickly.

Plaque Paste

This plaque paste can be used in the same ways as pastillage, and is less expensive to make as it doesn't require gum tragacanth.
This paste can be rolled very thinly, but it dries very quickly, even in wet weather.

1 teaspoon powdered gelatine
6 teaspoons water
250g (8oz/1½ cups) icing sugar
2 heaped teaspoons Tylose powder
½ heaped teaspoon cream of tartar

1 Dissolve the gelatine in the water as described in step 2 of the Pastillage recipe.

2 Sift the sugar, Tylose powder and cream of tartar together, make a well and add the gelatine. Stir quickly and, when bound, start kneading into a smooth, pliable paste.

Acknowledgements

The author would like to thank the following for supplying equipment for photography:

Orchard Products
(cutters)
15 Hallyburton Road,
Hove,
Sussex

Sugarflair Colours Ltd
(colours and dusts)
Brunel Road,
Manor Trading Estate,
Benfleet,
Essex, SS7 4PS

Original Sugarcraft Designs
(cake stands)
3 Anker Lane,
Stubbington,
Fareham,
Hants, PO14 3HF

J F Renshaw Ltd
(Regalice sugarpaste)
Crown Street,
Liverpool, L8 7RF

The publishers would like to thank the following suppliers:

Cake Art Ltd
Venture Way,
Crown Estate,
Priorswood,
Taunton, TA2 8DE

Guy, Paul and Co. Ltd
Unit B4,
Foundry Way,
Little End Road,
Eaton Socon,
Cambs., PE19 3JH

Squires Kitchen
Squires House,
3 Waverley Lane,
Farnham,
Surrey, GU9 8BB

**Anniversary House
(Cake Decorations) Ltd**
Unit 16,
Elliott Road,
West Howe Industrial Estate,
Bournemouth, BH11 8LZ

Sugar Inspirations

SUGAR INSPIRATIONS is a new collection of attractive books designed to expand your repertoire of sugarcraft techniques. Full of new ideas and lavishly illustrated, each book provides clear step-by-step instructions that guarantee good results.

WEDDING FLOWERS explains exactly how to make some of the most popular sugar flowers and how to use them in beautiful wedding cake decorations, including:

- Cake-top ornaments
- Shower and reverse curve bouquets
- Victorian posy

- Flowers ranging from simple stephanotis to elegant orchids
- Basic recipes and expert advice on choosing equipment

Other books in the series:

ANNIVERSARY CAKES

FOLDS & FRILLS

ISBN 1-85391-452-5

£4.99 UK

9 781853 914522 >

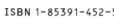